SCIENCE SLEUTHS

MEASURE IT!

CRYSTAL SIKKENS

Crabtree Publishing Company

www.crabtreebooks.com

SCIENCE SLEUTHS

?

To my beautiful daughter, Hailey Joy Sikkens,
who has brought so much joy and happiness to my life. All my love.

Author
Crystal Sikkens

Publishing plan research and development
Reagan Miller

Editor
Kathy Middleton

Indexer
Kathy Middleton

Photo research
Crystal Sikkens
Samara Parent

Design
Samara Parent

Print and production coordinator
Margaret Amy Salter

Prepress technician
Tammy McGarr

Photographs
iStock: front cover, p. 19; p. 21 (scales); p. 22 (scale)
Shutterstock: © dcwcreations p. 14 (both)
Thinkstock: p. 20 (left); p. 22 (middle right)

All other images by Shutterstock

Library and Archives Canada Cataloguing in Publication

Sikkens, Crystal, author
    Measure it! / Crystal Sikkens.

(Science sleuths)
Includes index.
Issued in print and electronic formats.
ISBN 978-0-7787-1540-5 (bound).--ISBN 978-0-7787-1544-3 (pbk.).--
ISBN 978-1-4271-1592-8 (pdf).--ISBN 978-1-4271-1588-1 (html)

    1. Measurement--Juvenile literature. 2. Metric system--
Juvenile literature. 3. Science--Methodology--Juvenile literature.
I. Title.

QA465.S55 2015   j530.8   C2015-901524-3
                                    C2015-901525-1

Library of Congress Cataloging-in-Publication Data

Sikkens, Crystal, author.
  Measure it! / Crystal Sikkens.
    pages cm. -- (Science sleuths)
  Includes index.
  ISBN 978-0-7787-1540-5 (reinforced library binding : alk. paper) --
ISBN 978-0-7787-1544-3 (pbk. : alk. paper) --
ISBN 978-1-4271-1592-8 (electronic pdf : alk. paper) --
ISBN 978-1-4271-1588-1 (electronic html : alk. paper)
1. Scientific apparatus and instruments--Juvenile literature. 2. Measurement--
Juvenile literature. 3. Science--Methodology--Juvenile literature. 4. Scientists--
Juvenile literature. I. Title.

Q185.3.S55 2015
502.8--dc23
                                     2015008985

Crabtree Publishing Company

Printed in the U.S.A./062015/CJ20150512

www.crabtreebooks.com   1-800-387-7650

Published in Canada
Crabtree Publishing
616 Welland Ave.
St. Catharines, Ontario
L2M 5V6

Published in the United States
Crabtree Publishing
PMB 59051
350 Fifth Avenue, 59th Floor
New York, New York 10118

Published in the United Kingdom
Crabtree Publishing
Maritime House
Basin Road North, Hove
BN41 1WR

Published in Australia
Crabtree Publishing
3 Charles Street
Coburg North
VIC 3058

CONTENTS

Observing exactly 4

The metric system 6

Length, height, and width 8

Comparing measurements 10

Measuring volume 12

Capacity 14

Taking temperature 16

Collecting data 18

Measuring mass 20

The right tool 22

Learning more 23

Glossary 24

Index 24

OBSERVING EXACTLY

Scientists are people who study the **natural world**. They ask questions and **observe**, or look carefully, to learn more about things around them. When people observe, they gather information using their senses of sight, smell, taste, hearing, and touch. Scientists use what they learn to answer questions. But sometimes they need information that is an exact measure, something we cannot get using just our senses.

The natural world is all the living and nonliving things around us.

You use your nose to find out what a flower smells like. You use your eyes to see what colors are on a butterfly.

TOOLS TO OBSERVE

You can use your sense of touch to find out whether the water in a pool is warmer in the morning or the afternoon. But what if you wanted to find out exactly how much warmer? You would have to use a measuring tool to answer your question. Scientists use measuring tools to make **observations** they cannot make using only their senses.

This scientist is using a measuring tool called a tape measure. With the tape measure he can find out exactly how tall each plant is.

THE METRIC SYSTEM

Hailey and her sister Erin share a room. They want to find out how long their room is. Hailey uses her shoes to measure the length of the room. She uses 20 shoes. Erin measures with her shoes and only uses 15. "Why did we get different measurements?" Hailey asks. Erin realizes it is because their shoes are not the same size.

If people measure with objects that are not the same size, they will get different measurements.

ON THE SAME PAGE

To make sure everyone is measuring the same way, scientists all around the world use only one system of measurement. It is called the **metric system**. Each measurement in the metric system has a number and a **unit**. A unit is a set size or quantity. Units have different names for different kinds of measurements.

LENGTH, HEIGHT, AND WIDTH

Meters (m), centimeters (cm), and millimeters (mm) are examples of metric units used to measure length, height, or width. Measuring tools with these metric units can be used to find out how long, tall, or wide something is, or how far away an object is.

One millimeter is about the thickness of a dime.

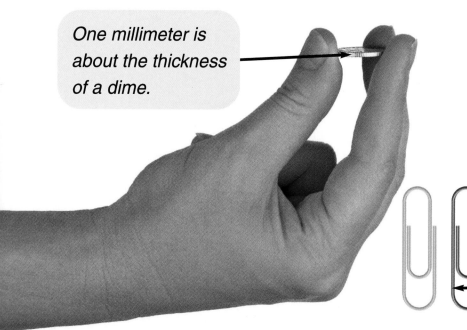

One meter is about the height of a doorknob from the floor.

One centimeter is about the width of a paper clip.

TERRIFIC TOOLS

A ruler is a tool used to measure small objects with straight lines. A meter stick measures longer objects with straight lines. A tape measure can bend. It is used to measure around an object. Some tape measures can be made longer to find out how far away something is.

EXPLORE IT!

?

Look at the picture above. Which measuring tool is being used? How do you know?

HOW TO MEASURE USING A RULER

1. Put the object next to the ruler. Be sure one end of the object lines up where the "0" would be on the ruler.

2. Next, look for the number that lines up with the other end of the object. This pencil is 15 centimeters long. Write this measurement as 15 cm.

COMPARING MEASUREMENTS

Scientists can use measurements to compare objects or put them in a specific order. Measuring the length of different objects can help scientists find out which object is the longest and by how much. Then they can put the objects in order from shortest to longest or longest to shortest.

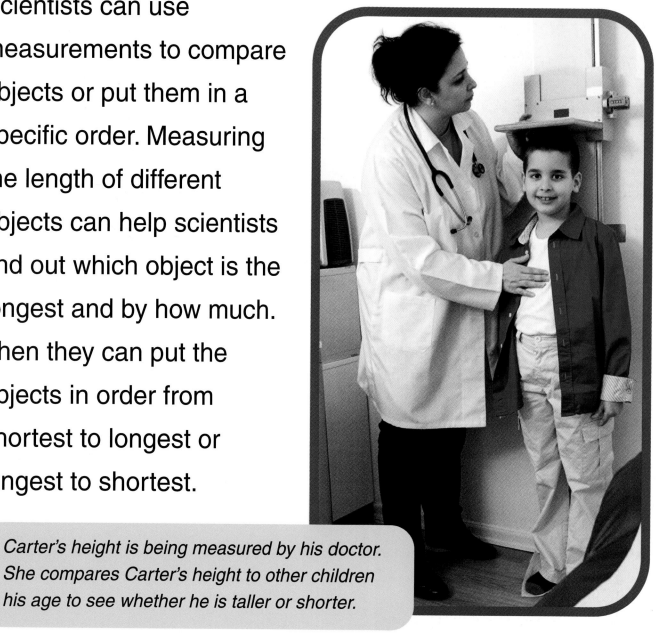

Carter's height is being measured by his doctor. She compares Carter's height to other children his age to see whether he is taller or shorter.

TRACKING TREES

Carter wanted to find out which tree would grow the tallest in one year. He planted a maple tree, a birch tree, a cedar tree, and an oak tree on his family's farm. The trees were all the same size when he planted them. After one year, he used a meter stick to measure the height of each tree. Carter wrote the measurements in a chart.

EXPLORE IT!

?

Compare the heights of the trees in the chart below. Then list the trees in order from shortest to tallest. Which tree grew the tallest in one year?

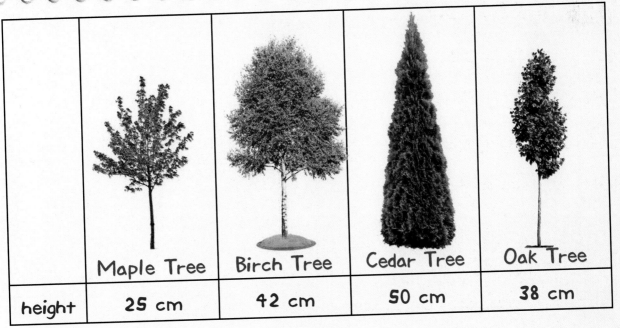

height	Maple Tree	Birch Tree	Cedar Tree	Oak Tree
	25 cm	42 cm	50 cm	38 cm

MEASURING VOLUME

Can you use a ruler to find out how much milk is in a glass? The amount of space something such as milk takes up in a container is called **volume**. You need different tools to measure volume. Have you ever helped bake a cake? You probably used a measuring cup to measure the liquid ingredients. A measuring cup measures volume. It has measurements printed on the side. Liquid volume is measured in units called liters (L). Liters can also be divided into smaller units called milliliters (mL).

This carton holds 1 liter of milk.

measuring cup

graduated cylinder

beaker

Scientists also use beakers and graduated cyclinders to measure, stir, mix, and heat liquids. These tools show volume measurements on the side.

USING A GRADUATED CYLINDER

1. Pour a liquid into a graduated cylinder on a table.

2. Wait until the liquid is still.

3. Bend down so your eyes are at the same level as the top of the liquid. You will see that the liquid curves up the sides of the cylinder slightly. Look at the line on the cylinder that is at the same level as the bottom of the liquid's curve. The number next to that line shows the volume of liquid inside.

The lines on this graduated cylinder go up by one unit. The liquid in this graduated cylinder reaches the line at 46 mL.

EXPLORE IT!

?

Which of these two pictures shows the correct way to read the measurement for liquid volume? Why?

CAPACITY

Capacity is the total volume that a container can hold. Containers come in many different shapes and sizes. The juicebox container below shows it has a capacity of 125 mL. The larger container beside it shows it has a capacity of 325 mL. Not all containers have their capacity written on them. To find the capacity of some containers, you have to measure the total amount of liquid they hold.

FINDING CAPACITY

You will need:

two containers   **water**   **measuring cup**

1. Find two small containers in your home that are different shapes, such as a short, wide container and a tall, thin one.

2. Just by looking at them, make a **prediction**, or guess, about which container you think holds the most liquid.

3. Test your prediction by filling each container with water. Pour the liquid from one container into a measuring cup. Read the measurement. Pour out the water and do the same for the other container.

What is the capacity of each container? Which container holds the most liquid? Was your prediction correct?

TAKING TEMPERATURE

Temperature is a measure of how hot or cold something is. A thermometer is a tool that measures temperature. Scientists measure temperature in units called degrees Celsius, or °C for short. Most thermometers are made up of a glass tube with red or blue liquid inside.

The liquid rises up the tube when the temperature gets warmer and moves down the tube when it gets cooler.

Celcius is a metric measure. In the United States, outdoor temperature is usually measured in degrees Fahrenheit, or °F. Many thermometers show both °C and °F.

HOW HOT? HOW COLD?

A thermometer outside your home can tell you what the temperature is outdoors. On a summer day it might reach a sweaty 30°C. On a winter day it might be a snowy -10°C. If you see ice outside your window, it means water has frozen. Water freezes at 0°C. It boils at 100°C.

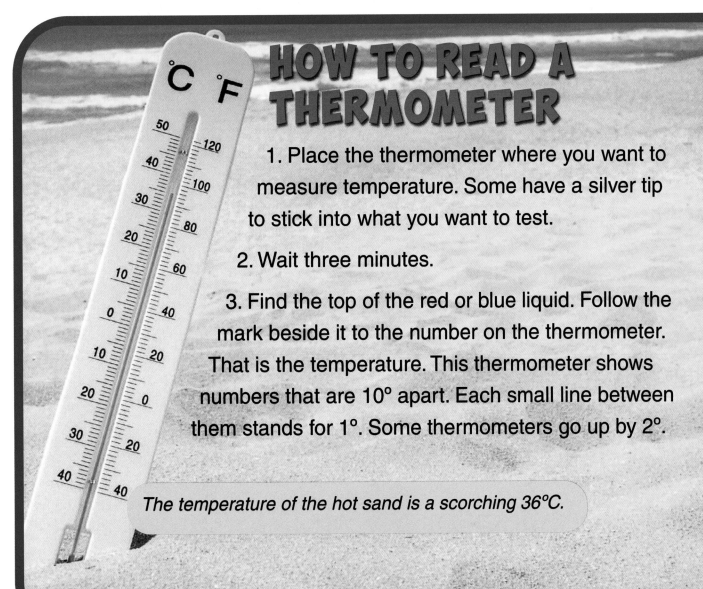

HOW TO READ A THERMOMETER

1. Place the thermometer where you want to measure temperature. Some have a silver tip to stick into what you want to test.

2. Wait three minutes.

3. Find the top of the red or blue liquid. Follow the mark beside it to the number on the thermometer. That is the temperature. This thermometer shows numbers that are 10° apart. Each small line between them stands for 1°. Some thermometers go up by 2°.

The temperature of the hot sand is a scorching 36°C.

COLLECTING DATA

Taking measurements is an important way for scientists to gather **data**. Data is information that is collected to help scientists answer questions. They use the data to compare things or find **patterns**. A pattern is something that repeats or grows larger or smaller by a set number each time. Patterns can help scientists make predictions.

Day	Time	Pool Temperature
Monday	8:00 am	22°C
Tuesday	8:00 am	24°C
Wednesday	8:00 am	26°C
Thursday	8:00 am	28°C
Friday	8:00 am	30°C

Gabriela wants to predict what the water temperature will be in her pool each day. She records the data she collected in a notebook.

POOL PATTERNS

Each day at the same time, Gabriela used a thermometer to measure the temperature of the water in her pool. She compared her data after five sunny days and found a pattern. Gabriela noticed that the temperature of the water got 2 degrees warmer each day.

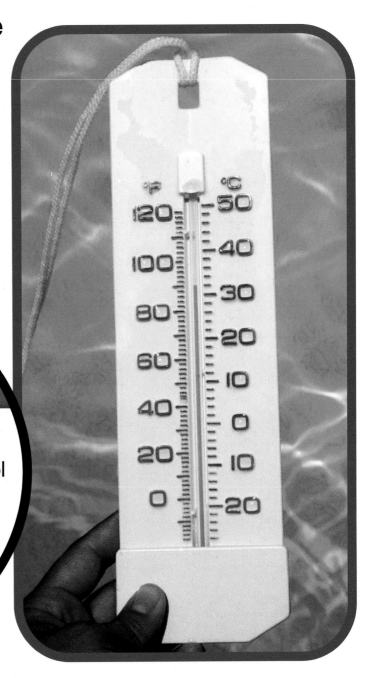

EXPLORE IT!

?

Following the pattern of the pool temperatures, can you predict what the temperature of Gabriela's pool will be on Saturday?

MEASURING MASS

Everything around us is made of material called **matter**. Matter can be anything that takes up space. The amount of matter in an object is called **mass**. A heavy object has more mass than a light object. An object's mass can be measured using a tool called a **balance**.

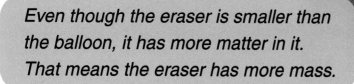

Even though the eraser is smaller than the balloon, it has more matter in it. That means the eraser has more mass.

BALANCE BASICS

You can observe two objects by picking them up and feeling which one is heavier. A balance helps you compare these objects and get a more exact measurement. Objects are placed on opposite sides on a balance. The object that sinks lower has more mass. The side holding the object with less mass will be higher.

EXPLORE IT!

?

Look at the balances below. List the objects in order from least amount of mass to most amount of mass.

apple

tennis ball

rock

apple

THE RIGHT TOOL

Read the problems below. Which measuring tool is needed to find the correct measurements?

1. Mary is buying a new skirt and she needs to find out the width of her waist.

2. Henry is making soup. He needs to add 1 liter of water.

3. Rahim is helping his mom cook chicken for dinner. The chicken is cooked when it reaches 80°C.

4. Katie is making a bird house. She needs a piece of wood that is 20 cm wide and 25 cm long.

5. Muhammad is going on a hiking trip. He needs to pack a lunch that is light to carry. He has to find out whether a sandwich or a salad would be lighter to carry.

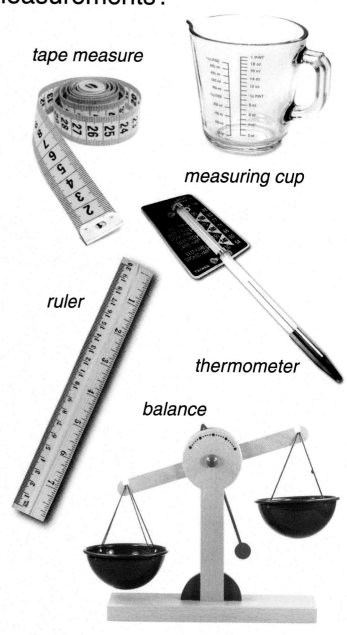

tape measure

measuring cup

ruler

thermometer

balance

LEARNING MORE

BOOKS

The Metric System by Paul Challen. Crabtree Publishing Company, 2010.

What is temperature? by Robin Johnson. Crabtree Publishing Company, 2013.

Measuring Volume by Beth Bence Reinke. Cherry Lake Publishing, 2013.

Measuring Length by Darice Bailer. Cherry Lake Publishing, 2013.

Balances by Adele D. Richardson. Capstone Press, 2004.

WEBSITES

This website explains how to measure using a ruler and a tape measure. It also includes an activity to practice measuring items in your home.
www.mathsisfun.com/activity/ discover-lengths.html

Learn more about measuring volume using milliliters and liters at this interesting website.
www.mathsisfun.com/measure/ metric-volume.html

Check out this website to learn more about the metric system and measuring temperature.
http://science.jrank.org/kids/pages /190/Measurement-Tools.html

GLOSSARY

Note: Some boldfaced words are defined where they appear in the text.

balance (BAL-uh-ns) noun A tool used to measure mass

capacity (kuh-PAS-i-tee) noun The total volume that a container can hold

data (DAT-uh) noun Facts and information collected by observations

mass (mas) noun The amount of matter in an object

metric system (ME-trik SIS-tuh m) noun A system of measurement based on meters and kilograms

natural world (NACH-er-uhl WURLD) noun All living and non-living things in the world

observe (ob-ZURV) verb To gather information by using your senses

observations (ob-zur-VEY-shuhnz) noun Information learned by using your senses or measuring

patterns (PAT-ernz) noun Something that repeats or increases or decreases by a set amount

predictions (pri-DIK-shuh-nz) noun Things that are said to happen based on observations

temperature (TEM-per-uh-cher) noun The measure of how hot or cold something is

volume (VOL-yoom) noun The amount of space something takes up

A noun is a person, place, or thing. A verb is an action word that tells you what someone or something does.

INDEX

balance 20, 21, 22
beaker 12
capacity 14–15
data 18, 19
graduated cylinder 12, 13
mass 20–21
measuring cup 12, 15, 22

measuring tools 5, 8, 9, 12, 16, 22
meter stick 9, 11
metric system 7
observations 4, 5, 19, 21
patterns 18, 19
predictions 15, 18

ruler 9, 22
senses 4, 5
tape measure 9, 22
temperature 16–17, 19
thermometer 16–17, 19, 22
units 7, 8, 12, 16
volume 12–13, 14